Muscular Dystrophy

Revised Edition

GAIL LEMLEY BURNETT

*Expert Reviews by Stephen D. Rioux, M.D.,
and Brenda Wong, M.D.*

Enslow Publishers, Inc.

40 Industrial Road	PO Box 38
Box 398	Aldershot
Berkeley Heights, NJ 07922	Hants GU12 6BP
USA	UK

http://www.enslow.com

Dedicated to families living with muscular dystrophy

Acknowledgments
With thanks to:
Stephen D. Rioux, M.D., Director of Muscular Dystrophy Clinics in Maine and pediatric neurologist, for his advice and review of this book.
Scott and Louise Parker, Michael Norton, and their families for their willingness to share their stories.

Printed in the United States of America. This is a revised edition of Muscular Dystrophy ©1996.

Library of Congress Cataloging-in-Publication Data
Burnett, Gail Lemley.
 Muscular dystrophy / Gail Lemley Burnett; expert review by Stephen D. Rioux/ Rev. ed.
  p. cm. —— (Health watch)
Includes bibliographical references and index.
Summary: Discusses the cause, symptoms, and treatment of muscular dystrophy and examines research into treatment and a possible cure.
 ISBN 0-7660-1651-X
 1. Muscular dystrophy—Juvenile literature. [1. Muscular dystrophy.
 2. Diseases.] I. Rioux, Stephen D. II. Title. III. Health watch (Berkeley Heights, N.J.)
  RC935.M7 B87 2000
  616.74'8—dc21
10 9 8 7 6 5 4 3 2 1

00-008401

To Our Readers:
All Internet addresses in this book were active and appropriate when we went to press. Any comments or suggestions can be sent by e-mail to Comments@enslow.com or to the address on the back cover.

Illustration and Photo Credits:
Courtesy of Muscular Dystrophy Association: pp. 1, 4, 12, 20, 21, 25, 37, 38; © Carl D. Walsh: pp. 6, 9, 15, 24; © Jill K. Gregory: p. 18; courtesy of Canine Companions: p. 28; © PhotoDisc, Inc.: p. 31.

Cover Illustrations:
Large photo, top and bottom insets: courtesy of Muscular Dystrophy Association.

Contents

A child with muscular dystrophy enjoys time with a camp counselor. "I do more than a lot of able-bodied people I know," says David Klock, a man with the disease.

Chapter 1

Two Families

M ichael Norton began falling down a lot after he learned to walk. His legs were stiff and he began to walk with a waddle. Because Michael was frequently sick, he was tested by several doctors.

When he was four years old, a test showed that Michael had a very high amount of a certain muscle **enzyme** in his blood. Enzymes are substances that speed up particular chemical reactions in the body. The high levels of the enzyme in Michael's blood were a sign that he had a form of **muscular dystrophy (MD).**

Muscular dystrophy is a disease that causes slow weakening of the muscles. It is an inherited disease, passed down from parents to children. The kind of MD Michael had, **Duchenne muscular dystrophy**, is the most common form of MD that affects children. It was named for a French doctor, Guillaume Duchenne, who wrote about the disease in 1868. Almost everyone who has Duchenne MD is a boy.

Children with Duchenne MD usually learn to walk

Michael Norton has muscular dystrophy. His mother massages his legs to keep them loose during therapy.

normally. Then, at ages three to five, they start having problems. Their leg muscles and pelvises become weak. Their weak legs often cause what doctors call a "waddling gait," which makes them sway from side to side when they walk. By the time they are twelve or thirteen, most boys with Duchenne are in wheelchairs.

As Michael grew, it became more difficult for him to go up and down stairs. But he continued to walk without **leg braces**. His parents massaged and stretched his leg muscles twice a week to help strengthen them.

Michael is smart and has always attended regular school. He likes to play with his younger brother, John, who does not have MD. Michael learned to ride a bike and played Tee-ball when he was younger. By the time he was ten, though, Michael had to use a wheelchair most of the time because his legs were so weak. His muscles tighten, or contract, because he can't move them. Surgery has helped with this problem, but tight muscles still bother Michael.

Now age twelve, Michael enjoys swimming, an activity that doesn't require strong leg muscles. He goes to the pool at least once a week. He also likes to draw. Like many children his age, Michael spends a lot of time playing computer games.

Every summer, Michael attends a camp run by the **Muscular Dystrophy Association (MDA)**, where he can play with other children who have MD. His mother, Suzan Norton, says Michael enjoys this chance to be on his own since he needs more help from his parents than most other twelve-year-old boys.

Michael has to be careful during flu season. A cold or the flu can be dangerous for him because of his disease. He gets flu shots every year.

Like most families touched by MD, Michael's family works hard to live as normal a life as possible. They want Michael to continue attending regular school and do things that other children do.

The Parkers' Story

Some families have a harder time than the Nortons because a muscle disease affects more than one family member. That is the case with the Parker family. Scott Parker and his mother, Louise Parker, both have **myotonic dystrophy**, a rare muscle disease closely related to muscular dystrophy. Myotonic dystrophy used to be known as the most common type of muscular dystrophy among adults. Now it is classified in the same family of diseases as muscular dystrophy and shares many of the same symptoms as MD.

When Scott Parker was born, he looked like a normal, healthy baby. But something wasn't right. His mother, Louise, could tell by the way he acted. Scott's older brother, who was adopted, had been alert as an infant. But Scott, she said, seemed limp and "just slept for six months after he was born."

Because he didn't move around much, he gained more weight than an average baby. But his doctors weren't too concerned, yet. When Scott started to walk, both his mother and his father, James, became more worried. Scott tried to walk on tiptoe. Instead of falling down on his bottom like other babies, Scott stiffened and fell straight back. He often bumped his head on the floor.

That was when the doctors decided to test Scott. The tests showed Scott had myotonic dystrophy. His muscles would keep getting weaker for the rest of his life.

Scott's parents had suspected their son had myotonic dystrophy even before the diagnosis. While she was pregnant, Louise Parker had had problems. Her muscles ached. When she walked or was active for a while, her legs felt stiff. Her two sisters and her brother had had the same problems years earlier.

"The minute I'd sit down, I'd have the stiffness back again," she recalled years later.

Doctors at first said her legs hurt because of her pregnancy, but Louise believed it was something else. The condition continued after Louise gave birth. From her own symptoms and Scott's, she knew that she and her son were

Scott Parker takes part in a music therapy and enrichment exercise at the Cerebral Palsy Center in Portland, Maine, where he attends school.

going to be like her sisters and her brother. Doctors had already told them that they had a rare form of disease related to MD. It seemed to run in the family.

Compared with many families with muscular dystrophy, Louise Parker's family has been lucky. The form of the disease they share takes a long time to worsen. It usually starts when a person is between the ages of twenty and forty. (Scott's illness, however, began when he was still a baby.) Those who have this form of muscle disease can live to be at least sixty or seventy.

Almost twenty years after the doctor told the Parkers of Scott's diagnosis, Louise and Scott Parker could both still walk with help. Louise needed someone to help her rise to a standing position and had to have rails or someone's arm to hold onto when she walked. She still went grocery shopping with her husband. She held on to the cart for support.

This form of the disease gets worse slowly. It stays the same for months at a time. Then "all of a sudden, you notice something else you can't do," Louise said. She put off using a wheelchair as long as she could, but she finally had to use one when she could no longer walk.

Scott will probably have a harder time because he has congenital myotonic dystrophy, which means he had the condition at birth. Unlike most people with muscular dystrophy, Scott has mild mental retardation. Now in his twenties, he reads about as well as a fourth-grader.

So far, Scott can walk with leg braces. He can also ride a bicycle and a horse. He doesn't like to talk about his disease. For several years, he went to a special school for physically handicapped children in Portland, Maine, near the family's home in Waterboro. He has held some part-time jobs. After graduation he went to work in the greenhouse at the school, where he stocked shelves and did other jobs.

Louise Parker, in her fifties at the time and weak from the disease, said she and her son weren't ready to lie down and be sick. She and Scott did as many things for themselves as they could. Whenever possible, Mrs. Parker worked in her garden, went grocery shopping, and did household chores. Scott goes to work, rides his bike, and takes horseback riding lessons.

It's important, Mrs. Parker said, not to accept limitations. "You have to fight it every step of the way." How muscular dystrophy and related diseases affect a person's life, she added, "depends on whether you give up or not." The Parkers refused to give up.

Chapter 2

What Is Muscular Dystrophy?

Each time people move, they use muscles. Even when people aren't moving, muscles play an important role. There are more than five hundred large and small muscles throughout the body. They control everything from breathing to kicking a soccer ball.

There are two basic kinds of muscles—voluntary and involuntary. **Voluntary muscles** are the ones people move on purpose. The muscles in a person's legs, used each time he or she walks or runs, are voluntary muscles. These muscles are also called skeletal muscles. They are connected to the bones that they help to move.

Involuntary muscles work whether a person thinks about them or not. They include the heart, which beats on its own, and the muscles that help move the food one eats through the intestines. A person doesn't have to tell the muscles to do their job. They just do it.

In muscular dystrophy, the voluntary muscles become

weak and break down. This happens over a period of years—sometimes many years, sometimes only a few. The muscles become weaker and flatter, so the person can do less and less with them.

As the disease worsens, the person has trouble moving the muscles affected by MD. Some kinds of muscular dystrophy affect the leg muscles. Other kinds affect the arm muscles. Still others affect the muscles of the face. In some cases, the disease eventually spreads to almost all the muscles in the body.

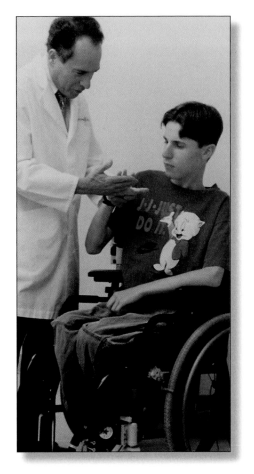

A doctor examines a boy with muscular dystrophy.

After a person has had MD for many years, the muscle weakness can spread to involuntary muscles. The disease can affect the heart and the lungs. But that doesn't happen with everyone who gets the disease.

Muscular dystrophy is a rare condition. Doctors estimate that two hundred fifty thousand people in the United States have MD. Duchenne muscular dystrophy, the most common type in children, affects one in thirty-five hundred boys and almost no girls.

Types of Muscular Dystrophy

Doctors have identified at least nine types of muscular dystrophy and several types of related muscular diseases. Some forms start in childhood, some during young adulthood, and others in old age. Some break down muscles quickly, while others take a long time. Different forms of MD affect different parts of the body.

All forms of MD have one thing in common—they are all **genetic diseases**. That means they are passed on within families, from parents to children.

Duchenne Muscular Dystrophy

Duchenne muscular dystrophy, the most common form of muscular dystrophy in children, is the kind Michael Norton has.

Children with Duchenne MD usually start having difficulty walking at ages three to five. They often walk with a waddle because their legs are weak. When they get older, Duchenne children often have curved backs, a condition called **scoliosis**. Their legs often look chubby because fat fills in where muscle is supposed to be.

Duchenne muscular dystrophy almost always affects boys. This form of the disease gets worse more quickly than many other kinds of MD. Most boys with Duchenne must use wheelchairs by the time they reach their teens. Their muscles keep getting weaker. Later, their breathing and their lungs—which are controlled by involuntary muscles—are affected. Because of these problems, most people with Duchenne MD die before they turn thirty.

That's one reason researchers are looking so hard to find a cure for this form of muscular dystrophy. People who raise money to fight MD, like comedian Jerry Lewis, spend a lot of time talking about Duchenne MD. This is the disease most people think of when they hear the words muscular dystrophy.

Becker Muscular Dystrophy

Becker muscular dystrophy is like Duchenne, except it is less severe and often begins later in life. Some people are already in their twenties when they get Becker MD. It affects the same parts of the body as Duchenne and in the same ways. But it takes much longer to get worse. Boys and young men with Becker can live longer than those with Duchenne.

Myotonic Dystrophy

Myotonic dystrophy, also known as Steinert's disease, can cause a slow weakening of muscles in the face, hands, feet, legs, and neck. Affected muscles become stiff, especially after they're used. This is the type the Parkers have.

Myotonic dystrophy usually starts between the ages of twenty and forty, but it also appears in childhood. People can live for many years with this disease. As with other forms of muscle diseases, people with myotonic dystrophy feel weak. Their legs and arms are likely to be thin, because their muscles get smaller and weaker as the disease progresses.

Louise Parker's disease weakened her legs, arms, back,

Scott Parker, who has myotonic dystrophy, is aided by his physical therapist, Barbara Gould, in an exercise to improve his body mechanics.

and lungs. She lost her balance easily and tripped over small things. Then she had a hard time getting up. Swallowing and chewing sometimes became difficult for her. And, at times, her heart raced.

The leg braces Scott Parker wears prevent him from walking on tiptoe and falling down. He has some problems keeping his balance. Like his mother, he is thin.

Scott's symptoms took twenty years to develop. For the first several years after being diagnosed with the disease, he could walk without braces or support. His mother had a similar experience with the disease.

Myotonic dystrophy is passed on by certain **genes**—the coded material we inherit from our parents. Children of a parent with the gene for myotonic dystrophy have a 50 percent chance of inheriting that gene. Anyone who inherits the gene will have the disease.

Doctors have recently discovered something interesting about myotonic dystrophy. Unlike most other genetic diseases, it can get worse from one generation to the next. The gene that causes it can change between parent and child.

Limb-girdle Muscular Dystrophy

Limb-girdle muscular dystrophy mainly affects the muscles of the pelvic area at the top of the legs (the pelvic girdle). Both children and adults can get the disease, but it is usually worse when it starts at an early age.

Symptoms are similar to those of Duchenne and Becker MD, but people with limb-girdle MD usually live longer. This form of MD is passed on to both boys and girls. People can carry the gene without having the disease.

Rarer Forms of Muscular Dystrophy

There are five other forms of muscular dystrophy. The most common of the five types is listed first; the least common is listed last.

❖ **Facioscapulohumeral:** **Facioscapulohumeral MD** usually affects the face and shoulders first. Patients may have trouble raising their arms over their heads or doing simple things like closing their eyes tightly or puffing their cheeks. Over time, the disease usually weakens the muscles in the torso and the legs. Twenty percent of those affected end up in a wheelchair. This form of MD affects boys and girls. It most often starts in the teen years or young adulthood and gets worse slowly.

❖ **Congenital**: **Congenital MD** begins at birth and gets worse slowly, if at all. It can affect all parts of the body and can affect boys and girls. It weakens the muscles, and in the worst cases, babies are born with joint deformities. In other cases, though, the disease is very mild and does not worsen at all.

❖ **Oculopharyngeal**: Often the first symptom of **oculopharyngeal MD** is drooping eyelids, caused by a weakening of muscles in the face. This kind of MD usually begins in older men and women, ages forty to seventy, and gets worse slowly.

❖ **Distal**: **Distal MD** also affects adults. It usually affects the hands first, making it hard to pick up things. People's feet and legs may get weak later. This disease usually spreads slowly.

❖ **Emery-Dreifuss**: **Emery-Dreifuss MD** causes shortening of the muscles of the elbows, knees, shoulders, and ankles and, sometimes, an abnormal heartbeat. It affects boys only.

So far, scientists have found no cure for any form of muscular dystrophy.

Chapter 3

Who Gets Muscular Dystrophy?

M uscular dystrophy is not like a cold, the flu, or chicken pox. A person can't catch it from being near someone who has the disease.

Muscular dystrophy is a genetic disease. The only people who get genetic diseases are those whose parents pass on to them the gene or genes that cause such diseases.

Genes are the coded material that control what people

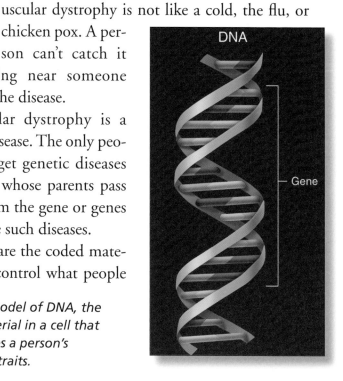

DNA

Gene

This is a model of DNA, the basic material in a cell that determines a person's inherited traits.

will be like. Genes determine the color of a person's eyes and hair. They direct whether people will look more like their fathers or their mothers. Genes are similar to a blueprint, which determines how a building will be constructed.

Sometimes genes also determine what kinds of diseases people will have. Genetic diseases are almost always passed on in one of three ways: by **dominant genes**, by **recessive genes**, or by **X-linked genes**.

Dominant Genes

For each gene a person inherits from his or her mother, a matching gene is inherited from that person's father. Those two genes—or sometimes a combination of genes—determine a child's traits. For example, if a boy gets a gene for brown eyes from his mother and a gene for blue eyes from his father, he will probably have brown eyes. That is because the gene for brown eyes—the dominant gene—is stronger than the gene for blue eyes—the recessive gene.

Diseases that are passed on through dominant genes, such as myotonic dystrophy, usually show up in each generation of a family. That's because everyone who inherits the defective gene from a parent will have the disease. It dominates over the matching, but normal, gene from the other parent.

Recessive Genes

Diseases passed on by recessive genes can catch families by surprise. That's because a recessive gene can hide in people

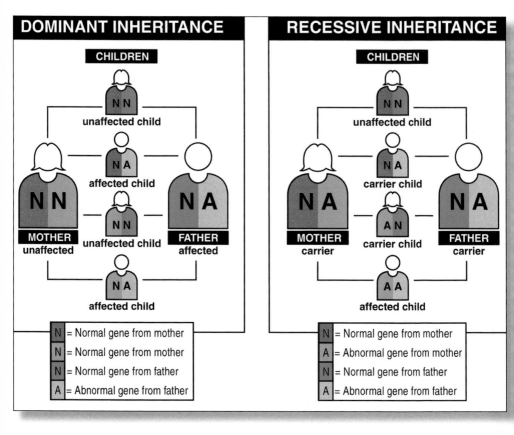

This chart shows how the gene for muscular dystrophy (A), is passed down from parents to children.

who inherit the gene. If they also inherit a matching gene that is normal, that normal gene dominates. So they don't get the disease. But they can pass it on to their children.

A child must inherit two recessive genes to have the disease. It works the same way for eye color and certain other traits. If a girl has blue eyes, chances are she got the genes for blue eyes from both her father and her mother. But both her parents could have brown eyes. They could each carry one gene for brown eyes and one gene for blue eyes.

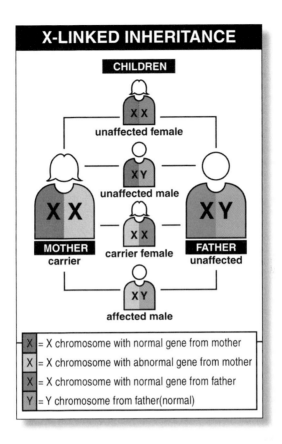

X-LINKED INHERITANCE

CHILDREN

XX
unaffected female

XY
unaffected male

XX
carrier female

XY
affected male

X X
MOTHER
carrier

X Y
FATHER
unaffected

X = X chromosome with normal gene from mother
X = X chromosome with abnormal gene from mother
X = X chromosome with normal gene from father
Y = Y chromosome from father(normal)

Conditions passed on by recessive genes are usually less common than those handed down through dominant genes. The kinds of muscular dystrophy that are passed on through recessive genes include limb-girdle and congenital muscular dystrophy.

X-linked Genes

Like hair color and other traits, a person's sex is determined by genetic information from one's parents. Each of us inherits two sex **chromosomes** (strings of genes): one from our mother and one from our father. Women have two X chromosomes, so every child they have—boy or girl—will inherit an X chromosome from the mother. Men, though, have an X chromosome and a Y chromosome. If a man passes along an X chromosome, the child will be a girl. If he passes along a Y chromosome, the child will be a boy.

Diseases like Duchenne MD almost always strike boys. The recessive gene that causes such diseases is on the X chromosome. In a girl who inherits the Duchenne gene, the faulty gene is dominated by the healthy gene on her other X chromosome. But boys have no other X chromosome. So if a boy inherits the gene from his mother, he will have the disease. Becker and Emery-Dreifuss are other X-linked forms of muscular dystrophy.

A common example of an X-linked condition is color blindness. Girls rarely have color blindness, but they can inherit the gene and pass it on to their children. Boys who get the gene, however, will have trouble telling some colors apart.

Sometimes a genetic disease is passed on by a parent who does not carry the gene. Something happens while the baby is forming, and the gene mutates, or changes.

For example, when Michael Norton, whose story is told in Chapter 1, was diagnosed with Duchenne MD, his mother's blood was studied. Doctors found out she did not carry the Duchenne gene. They told her that Michael's disease resulted from a mutation. Like many other diseases, it just happened, and doctors don't know why yet. Researchers are learning new things about inherited diseases all the time.

Living With Muscular Dystrophy

When today's grandparents were children, a boy like Michael Norton who became weak because of muscular dystrophy didn't have much chance to have fun. He would most likely have been put in a wheelchair, and his parents and other people would have waited on him. They might have helped him with the simplest tasks, like eating. He would have lost his strength faster because he wouldn't have been allowed to do anything for himself.

Today, therapists, doctors, and parents do everything they can to help children and adults with MD enjoy their lives. That includes letting them do things for themselves.

If a person lifted weights every day for a year, his or her arms would get stronger. In a way, the same thing is true of people with muscular dystrophy. The more they use their affected muscles, the stronger those muscles will remain.

That's one reason Michael and the Parkers continued to

Michael Norton prepares to hit the ball during a game of Tee-ball. His family encourages him to participate in as many activities as he can.

walk as long as they could before using wheelchairs. The longer people with MD can walk, the stronger they will be. When people with muscular dystrophy do need help, though, they can turn to many kinds of specialists.

Physical Therapists

Physical therapy helps patients stay in good physical shape. Physical therapists show people with muscular dystrophy how to do exercises that help the muscles and the spine. Most of the exercises involve some stretching of various muscles. In physical therapy, patients also practice walking normally, with their feet flat on the ground and their bodies straight.

A physical therapist shows a man who has a muscle disease how to do an exercise to help him improve his balance.

Occupational Therapists

Simple things can be hard to perform if a person's muscles are getting weaker all the time. People with muscular dystrophy often seek **occupational therapy**, where specialists provide training to help with everyday activities.

At a school like the one Scott Parker attended, occupational therapists encourage children with MD to dress and feed themselves, brush their teeth, and do other everyday tasks. If an older person's hand muscles are weakened by muscular dystrophy or related disease, an occupational therapist may help that person practice turning doorknobs or buttoning buttons.

Speech Therapists

Speech therapy is often recommended for patients with muscular dystrophy who have difficulty talking clearly. The muscles in the face and neck are sometimes affected by the disease. By having patients practice different sounds, speech therapists can help them improve their ability to talk.

Some problems caused by muscular dystrophy need special help. For example, patients who have trouble swallowing may be unable to eat, drink, and breathe properly. A speech therapist can help with swallowing problems by teaching patients new breathing techniques or tongue strengthening exercises that can help them to swallow.

Other Types of Help

Eventually, most people with the more serious kinds of muscular dystrophy have a hard time walking without some kind of help. When that happens, they use leg braces—hard plastic bands that strap onto the legs. The braces hold the legs steady when weakened muscles can't support the legs anymore. Braces are the closest thing to new muscles for an MD patient.

When leg braces are no longer enough, many people with MD use walkers. A walker is a metal frame that supports the body as the person takes steps. Later, patients may use motorized carts or wheelchairs. They can go many places in wheelchairs, but there are barriers. Stairs, heavy doors, or high curbs can be a stop sign for someone in a wheelchair.

Louise Parker walked with braces as long as she could because wheelchairs make life more difficult. Even with braces, she said, she sometimes encountered obstacles. Some people let heavy doors slam in her face; other people turned away when she fell and needed help getting on her feet.

But most people are helpful, and things are changing for the disabled. Schools and many other public places— like town halls and many stores, buses, and houses of worship—are required by law to have ramps alongside stairs and doors wide enough for wheelchairs to enter.

Since 1992, businesses with at least twenty-five workers have been required to remodel their buildings so handicapped people, including those in wheelchairs, can enter. The **Americans with Disabilities Act (ADA)** also forbids employers from discriminating because of physical disabilities. If people are qualified for jobs, for example, they can't be turned down just because they can't walk.

When the ADA was signed into law, one U.S. senator called it "the twentieth century Emancipation Proclamation." Like the act that freed the slaves, the ADA allowed people with disabilities to lead normal lives.

Some disabled people say this kind of progress is just as important as research to find cures for diseases like MD. If schools, stores, workplaces, and recreational areas are open to people in wheelchairs, then being in a wheelchair will be seen as a difference, not a disability.

Researchers are exploring new ways to help people with

A canine companion takes a break from the serious business of aiding his wheelchair-bound owner.

MD live on their own. A California group called Canine Companions for Independence trains dogs to do simple jobs for disabled people. Some children with muscular dystrophy use the dogs.

A canine helper can fetch a lunch bag, turn on lights, carry books, open doors, and retrieve things from high shelves. Like seeing-eye dogs, the helper dogs are allowed in places where pets wouldn't normally be permitted. They are allowed to go to school with their owners.

David Klock, a Pennsylvania man in his thirties who is in a wheelchair as a result of muscular dystrophy, has a helper dog, Candy. She opens doors, carries items, and helps him exercise. She goes with him to his job as an engineer at a United States Navy plant. Klock was diagnosed with facioscapulohumeral MD when he was twelve. Now, more than twenty years later, he says, "I do more than a lot of able-bodied people I know." Candy, his dog companion, helps.

Respect Is Important

According to Louise Parker, thinking positively can be a big help for people with muscular dystrophy. Louise always appreciated people who took the time to understand her disease. Louise's worst days occurred when people closed doors in her face. It was hard for her, too, when people talked to her husband but not to her, as if she were incapable of understanding what was being said. Louise said sometimes people seemed surprised when she told them she graduated from high school.

The best times, she said, were when people treated her with the respect and the dignity all humans deserve.

"There are lots of times I get disgusted," she said. But then she relished the summer mornings when she could get out in the yard and plant flowers—by herself.

Chapter 5

Muscular Dystrophy Research

S cientists are like detectives. For years they have been hunting for answers to questions about muscular dystrophy. What causes it? Why does one type of the disease attack muscles differently from another type? What can be done to treat or prevent the disease? Scientists have made some discoveries and are hot on the trail of others.

Beginning in 1986, researchers have found the genes or the approximate location of the genes responsible for most forms of MD. Finding the gene is a first step toward uncovering the mysteries surrounding a disease. Someday researchers hope their work will lead to a cure for muscular dystrophy.

One big breakthrough was the discovery of the gene responsible for Duchenne muscular dystrophy and Becker MD. Researchers learned that the normal gene tells the body to make a **protein** called **dystrophin**. Healthy muscles contain dystrophin, which helps them work.

Scientists learned that the mutated dystrophin gene doesn't do its job. In people with Duchenne, the body doesn't make dystrophin, and the muscles start to get weak while the person is still young. In people with Becker MD, the gene makes some dystrophin, but not enough.

Those discoveries led to tests that families with a history of either form of MD can take. Women can learn whether they carry the gene for Duchenne or Becker. Doctors can learn for sure whether a boy has Duchenne or Becker.

Researchers are working to find better ways to diagnose and treat disease. They hope someday to find cures.

A woman who knows she carries the Duchenne or Becker gene may decide not to have children. If she does get pregnant, she may have her baby's blood tested before the baby is born. Then she will know whether her baby will develop muscular dystrophy.

Other discoveries have led to a better understanding of how MD works. In 1992, scientists learned more about the way diseases are inherited. A parent with a genetic disease usually passes that same disease to his or her children. But with myotonic dystrophy, genes can change from one generation to the next. The children of a person with mild myotonic dystrophy may inherit a stronger version of the same disease. The problem genes may increase from one generation to the next.

That's what happened with the family of Louise Parker. Neither of her parents seemed to have myotonic dystrophy. Looking back, her father said he thought his aunt might have had the disease because of the strange way she walked. But she was never diagnosed by a doctor, and no one in the family knew about the disease then.

Doctors think Louise Parker's father had a mild form of MD. He passed it on to all four of his children. Each child had a worse case than the father. Louise's son, Scott, has a worse case than she has. While Louise did not get sick until she was in her thirties, Scott was sick at birth.

Better Methods of Diagnosis

It isn't always easy to diagnose the reason for muscle weakness. The sooner tests can show exactly what the problem is, the sooner good treatment can begin.

The first way a doctor decides whether someone has MD is by observing the person. The doctor watches the way the person walks, sits, and gets up from a chair. Usually a doctor tests the person's muscles to see why he or she is feeling weak or stiff.

Boys suspected of having Duchenne or Becker MD can be given a blood test to check for abnormally high levels of a muscle enzyme. In people with muscular dystrophy, the enzyme leaks out of muscle cells because the membranes that surround the cells have been damaged.

A test called an **electromyogram**, or **EMG**, records the way a person's muscles work. It prints a chart, like the pictures taken of heartbeats in electrocardiograms. Doctors can usually tell by looking at the chart whether a person has a muscle disorder. Another screening method used in muscular dystrophy is a **nerve conduction velocity test**. This test uses electrical impulses too, but the electrodes are placed on the skin. If the patient's test results are within normal range, the doctor knows that the patient's weakness is not due to a nerve disorder.

Another test that scientists have developed is called a **muscle biopsy**. In that test, a piece of muscle about the size of a fingertip is studied under a microscope. Healthy muscle looks quite different from muscle affected by MD. Sometimes muscle biopsies can show doctors which form of muscular dystrophy a person has.

Some new research into MD focuses on better ways to diagnose the disease. Doctors can now test the **DNA (deoxyribonucleic acid)**, the genetic material, of people suspected of having many forms of MD. The test shows whether the person has the abnormal gene that causes the disease.

Looking for a Cure

Scientists are working hard to find a cure for muscular dystrophy. Much of their attention is focused today on **gene therapy**. In gene therapy, healthy genes are injected into a person with MD. By doing this, scientists hope that the healthy genes will reproduce quickly and teach the patient's body to make the proteins and other materials it needs for healthy muscles.

In late 1999, the first human test of gene therapy was

conducted on a man in his thirties who has limb-girdle MD. It is still too early to tell whether the test will be safe and effective in treating muscular dystrophy.

Another area of research involves the use of **antibiotics** to treat some forms of MD. Researchers found that when rats with a particular kind of Duchenne were injected with high doses of the antibiotic **gentamicin**, their bodies started making dystrophin, the protein that helps produce healthy muscles. But this treatment needs much more research before it can be tried in humans. The large doses of gentamicin required in the treatment could cause serious kidney damage and deafness.

In 1990, researchers started testing a method they hoped would lead to an MD treatment. In the tests, healthy muscle cells that were growing were injected into the muscles of a person with MD. Scientists hoped the healthy cells would keep growing, making the weak muscles stronger.

Researchers are still conducting the tests, but the results have been disappointing. It is hard to put healthy cells in all the places where a person's muscles are weak. Everyone's body is different. When the cells from one person are put into another person, they can be rejected. The body of the person with muscular dystrophy can tell the difference between its own cells and someone else's. It wants to kick out the intruder cells.

Progress has been slow, but many scientists continue to work for a cure for muscular dystrophy. Someday, they may find it.

Chapter 6

Help and Hope

The Muscular Dystrophy Association is the major organization that raises funds to fight muscular dystrophy. It is one of the largest and best organized charities in the United States.

The MDA pays for research with the millions of dollars it raises each year. It also provides services to people with MD and their families. And it educates the public about muscular dystrophy.

The MDA was formed in 1950 by a group of parents who were hoping to find treatments or cures for their children's disease. At that time, according to the MDA, only one doctor in the United States had a practice devoted to fighting diseases like MD.

More than four hundred teams of scientists and doctors now use money from the MDA to study muscle diseases. Their discoveries have sometimes led to better understanding of diseases that have nothing to do with MD—like cataracts and Alzheimer's disease (a brain disease that destroys the ability to think, feel, remember, and care for oneself). They have also made major discoveries about Duchenne, Becker, and myotonic dystrophies.

In 1992 Edwin G. Krebs and Edmond H. Fischer, two scientists who had worked for years with the MDA, won the Nobel Prize in medicine. They were honored for their discovery of the way cells malfunction in diseases like MD. The Nobel Prize is one of the highest honors awarded to researchers.

The MDA runs about 230 clinics around the country. People with MD and their families receive a number of services at the clinics. People can be diagnosed there. Later, they can go to the clinics to get check-ups, flu shots, and therapy. Also, women who think they carry the gene for Duchenne or Becker MD can get tested. The clinics have wheelchairs, leg braces, and walkers for MD patients. The equipment is often free for patients who can't afford it.

Living with a **progressive disease** like MD—a disease that keeps getting worse—can be very hard on a family. Mothers, fathers, sisters, and brothers of patients can get counseling through MDA clinics. They are encouraged to talk about how they feel. For instance, a brother or sister of a child with MD may feel angry that the sick family member gets so much of their parents' attention.

The MDA runs nearly ninety summer camps for children with muscular dystrophy and related muscle diseases. There, young people can learn new skills, spend time outside, and get a break from their daily routines.

The MDA also publishes booklets that explain what muscular dystrophy is and what can be done to help patients. There are books for brothers and sisters about how it feels to have a sick family member.

Two boys enjoy their time together at a summer camp for children with muscular dystrophy.

In 1966 the MDA began holding telethons. Singers, dancers, and other entertainers perform on television, and people with MD talk about the disease while viewers are asked to call in with pledges of money. In 1999, the MDA telethon raised more than $53 million.

"Jerry's Kids"

Jerry Lewis is the MDA's national chairman. He has hosted the Labor Day Telethons since they began. His

Actor and comedian Jerry Lewis, national chairman of the Muscular Dystrophy Association, with Kelly Rose Mahoney, who served as goodwill ambassador for the organization.

name is so linked to MD that children with the disease are often called "Jerry's kids."

In the early 1990s, activists for the disabled complained that the telethon makes viewers feel sorry for people with MD instead of helping them understand and respect those with the disease. In response, the MDA made some changes. It has included more profiles of adults in its telethons. In 1992, it formed a committee of successful adults who have MD or other muscle diseases. Members of the National Task Force on Public Awareness who have muscular dystrophy include a number of successful professionals—a real estate consultant, a neurologist (a doctor who treats nerve diseases), the owner of a graphic arts firm, a college administrator, a woman who travels around the country talking about disabilities, and an electronics engineer with the United States Navy. Even Lewis's critics have agreed that the MDA does more than any other group to unlock the secrets of muscular dystrophy.

Help Available

Another group that has helped people with muscular dystrophy for many years is the Muscular Dystrophy Family Foundation, which provides services and equipment for those who need it. The foundation helps with home visits and organizes support groups for patients and their families. And it sponsors concerts by a musical group called Van Gogh. The group includes brothers Robby and Ricky Heisner, who both have MD.

The Shriners run a network of twenty-two Shriners Hospitals for Children around the country. The hospitals provide free help to children with physical disabilities, including muscular dystrophy. They offer physical and occupational therapy and perform surgery on children whose backs have become curved by muscular dystrophy.

Support groups can help people who are living with muscular dystrophy. The Facio-Scapulo-Humeral Society in Massachusetts assists people who have that rare disease. It also provides information about FSH and pushes for more research.

Families and friends can be the biggest help to people with muscular dystrophy. Children learn to do more for themselves if they are encouraged by others. Doing more makes them feel better about themselves. That is why programs like canine helpers and adaptive sports (games for children with disabilities) are so important.

The Muscular Dystrophy Association urges people to remember some things about those with MD:

- They didn't do anything wrong to get the disease; it just happened.
- Most can do anything other people can do with their heads and hands.
- Most are not retarded.
- Many people can live for decades with MD.
- People with MD, just like anyone else, need love, encouragement, and understanding.

Suzan Norton, the mother of MD patient Michael Norton, wants other parents to know that having a child with MD isn't as sad as they might think. She appreciates every day with Michael and has learned to live one day at a time.

And like any parent, she loves her son. "I wouldn't trade places with anybody," she said.

Louise Parker, who contributed to this book, died in 1995 from complications of muscular dystrophy.

Further Reading

Cheney, Glenn A. *Teens with Physical Disabilities: Real-Life Stories of Meeting the Challenge.* Berkeley Heights, N.J.: Enslow Publishers, Inc. 1995.

Corrick, James A. *Muscular Dystrophy.* Danbury, Conn.: Franklin Watts, 1992.

Edelson, Edward. *Genetics & Heredity.* New York: Chelsea House Publishers, 1991.

Emery, Alan E. *Muscular Dystrophy: The Facts.* New York: Oxford University Press, 1994.

Feinberg, Brian. *The Musculoskeletal System.* New York: Chelsea House Publishers, 1994.

Krementz, Jill. *How It Feels to Live with a Disability.* New York: Simon & Schuster, 1992.

Landa, Norbert, and Patrick A. Baeuerle. *Ingenious Genes: Microexplorers: Learning About the Fantastic Skills of Genetic Engineers and Watching Them at Work (Microexplorers Series).* New York: Barrons Juveniles, 1999.

Marshall, Elizabeth L. *The Human Genome Project : Cracking the Code Within Us.* Danbury, Conn.: Franklin Watts, 1997.

Parker, Steve. *The Skeleton and Muscular System (Human Body).* Austin, Tex.: Raintree/Steck Vaughn, 1997.

Sanders, Pete, and Steve Myers. *People With Disabilities.* Brookfield, Conn: Millbrook Press, 1998.

Siegel, Irwin. *Muscular Dystrophy in Children: A Guide for Families.* Hauppage, New York: Demos Medical Publishing, Inc., 1999.

Silverstein, Alvin, Robert Silverstein, and Virginia B. Silverstein. *The Muscular System.* New York: Twenty-First Century Books, 1995.

For More Information

The following is a list of organizations and Internet sites that deal with muscular dystrophy.

Organizations

Canine Companions for Independence
P.O. Box 446, Santa Rosa, CA 95402 (707) 577-1700, (800) 572-BARK; <http://www.caninecompanions. org>. This organization trains dogs to be helpers for disabled people, including those with MD.

Facio-Scapulo-Humeral Society
3 Westwood Road, Lexington, MA 02420; (781) 860-0501; <http://www.fshsociety.org>. Offers information about facioscapulohumeral MD and support for those who have it.

Muscular Dystrophy Association
3300 E. Sunrise Drive, Tucson, AZ 85718-3208, (800) 572-1717; <http://www.mdausa.org>. The major fund-raising and information organization for MD. Regional offices are in most states and are listed in the phone book.

Muscular Dystrophy Family Foundation
615 N. Alabama St., Suite 330, Indianapolis, IN 46204; (800) 544-1213, (317) 632-8255; <http:// www.mdff.org>. Provides MD information, services and financial assistance to families for equipment, and scholarships to children for summer programs.

Shriners Hospitals for Children
2900 Rocky Point Drive, Tampa, FL 33607-1460,
(813) 281-0300; <http://www.shrinershq.org/
Hospitals/index.html>. This national organization
operates hospitals that provide free services to children
with disabilities, including MD.

Internet Resources

<http://www.uwo.ca/biochem/DMD/Jesse.html>
Jesse's Journey—This site describes the 1995
wheelchair journey across Ontario, Canada, by a boy
with MD. There is now an annual—shorter—ride to
raise funds for MD. Web site sponsored by the
Foundation for Gene and Cell Therapy, P.O. Box
5099, London, Ontario, N6A 4M8; (519) 679-2828.

<http://www.geocities.com/capecanaveral/8676>
Haynes Family's Duchenne MD Information Page—
Information posted by the family of a South Carolina
boy with MD. The site has a specific focus on
Duchenne MD.

<http://www.parentdmd.org>
The Parent Project for MD Research—Includes a link
to a kids' page about MD with a chat room, message
board, kids' forum, and stories written by young
people with MD.

Glossary

Americans with Disabilities Act (ADA)—A federal law passed in 1992 that guarantees people with disabilities the right to jobs and access to public buildings.

antibiotic—A medication that kills germs.

Becker muscular dystrophy—A form of muscular dystrophy similar to Duchenne but that often starts later in life and takes longer to worsen. This type of muscular dystrophy affects boys only.

chromosome—A string of genes (*See* genes).

congenital muscular dystrophy—A type of muscular dystrophy that begins at birth.

distal muscular dystrophy—A mild form of muscular dystrophy that usually starts in adulthood.

DNA (deoxyribonucleic acid)—The coded material that determines a person's genetic traits. A person's DNA can be tested to find out if he or she has a genetic disease.

dominant gene—The stronger gene that usually controls or determines an inherited trait.

Duchenne muscular dystrophy—The most common childhood form of muscular dystrophy. It affects boys and usually leads to death before age thirty.

dystrophin—A protein found in healthy muscles. It is missing in people with muscular dystrophy.

electromyogram (EMG)—A test that records the way a person's muscles work.

Emery-Dreifuss muscular dystrophy—A rare form of muscular dystrophy that affects boys. It usually first weakens muscles in the upper body.

enzyme—A protein that speeds up certain chemical reactions in the body; for example, converting food into energy.

facioscapulohumeral muscular dystrophy—A slowly progressing form of muscular dystrophy that often affects face muscles and usually starts in the teen or young adult years.

genes—The coded material that determines how people will look and, sometimes, what illnesses they will get.

gene therapy—A treatment in which healthy genes are injected into a person with a disease, such as muscular dystrophy, that is caused by a defective gene.

genetic diseases—Illnesses that are passed on through families and are not contagious.

gentamicin—An antibiotic used in experimental treatment of muscular dystrophy in mice.

involuntary muscles—Muscles that work automatically and are not controlled by choice.

leg braces—Plastic supports that are worn on the legs of people with muscular dystrophy and some other diseases. They help support weak muscles.

limb-girdle muscular dystrophy—A form of muscular dystrophy that causes weakness mainly in the shoulder and hip areas and affects both males and females.

muscle biopsy—A test that examines a piece of muscle to determine if a person has muscular dystrophy.

muscular dystrophy (MD)—A genetic disease that causes slow weakening of the muscles.

Muscular Dystrophy Association (MDA)—The major fund-raising, educational, and research organization for muscular dystrophy.

myotonic dystrophy—A muscle disease closely related to muscular dystrophy, marked by muscle stiffness. It used to be classified as muscular dystrophy and was the most common form of the disease among adults.

nerve conduction velocity test—A screening method using electrical impulses that indicates whether the nerves are functioning properly.

occupational therapy—Treatment that helps people with everyday tasks, such as getting dressed.

oculopharyngeal muscular dystrophy—A form of muscular dystrophy that strikes older people and usually affects face muscles.

physical therapy—Treatment that helps people maintain muscle strength and flexibility.

progressive disease—A disease that gets worse over time.

proteins—Molecules that encourage growth, repair tissue, and perform other functions in the body. Enzymes are proteins.

recessive gene—The less powerful gene that usually stays hidden in the person who inherits it.

scoliosis—Curving of the backbone that can affect patients (boys and girls) with muscular dystrophy.

voluntary muscles—Muscles that are controlled by choice. In muscular dystrophy, these muscles become weak and break down.

x-linked gene—A gene that is on the X chromosome. Traits related to this type of gene, such as certain kinds of MD, are much more common in boys than girls.

Index